*New Directions - A Blueprint for Economic Renewal & Prosperity*

## Table of Contents

1. Introduction

3. The Challenge

6. The Agenda (including highlights)

8. Jobs, Training & Investment

8. Ontario Jobs, Adjustment & Training Secretariat

9. Job Creation Strategy

11. Adjustment and Training Strategy

12. Investment Strategy

22. Fiscal & Budgetary Policies

22. Taxation

25. Spending Controls

30. Reforming the Budgetary Process

32. Conclusion

# New Directions

## Volume One:

*A Blueprint for Economic Renewal and Prosperity in Ontario*

Prepared
by the

Ontario Progressive Conservative Caucus

Mike Harris
Leader

Legislative Building
Queen's Park
Toronto, Ontario

October 31, 1991

### New Directions - A Blueprint for Economic Renewal & Prosperity

Ontario is in trouble. Our economy is being battered by high taxation, high unemployment, and low productivity. Our social structure is stretched to the limit by soaring costs for health, education and welfare. The problems of crime and poverty seem to be growing faster than we can respond to them.

However, the foundations of our society are so strong that we still enjoy one of the highest standards of living of any people on the planet. Taking action now to address all of these complex problems can preserve our province as one of the best places to live in the world.

Our time is limited. As these economic and social pressures continue to build, it will become harder and harder to reverse the trend.

For these reasons, my caucus and I are presenting a series of papers dealing with the major problems and issues facing Ontarians and their government.

This paper (Volume One) addresses our economic problems. Renewing the economy is the first step towards resolution of social problems because without a strong economic base there are no jobs, no investment, and no tax base to fund social programs.

As well, our problems in resolving social ills are linked directly with a weak economy. When there is no opportunity for employment or prosperity, people cannot contribute to society economically and instead add their weight to the social burden carried by the rest of the population. On the other hand, when people have jobs and the confidence to invest in the economy, the size of that social burden is immensely reduced. The fewer people who *need* help, the more we *can* help them.

The proposals we are putting forward here are the beginning of a process to find answers to our most pressing problems. They are the result of input from many groups and individuals, but we look forward to hearing comments and suggestions from both the public and Ontario's other political parties.

*"...We still enjoy one of the highest standards of living of any people on the planet."*

*"The fewer people who need help, the more we can help them."*

*"Our economic problems are far too pressing and real to allow anyone the luxury of playing political games."*

This is not a political document. Our economic problems are far too pressing and real to allow anyone the luxury of playing political games. I truly believe that only a healthy economy can allow those at the lowest end of the economic scale to enjoy the full fruits of our society, and provide the highest standard of life for *all* the people of Ontario.

Yes, these are Conservative ideas, but they are also practical ideas based more on economic reality than on philosophy.

It is my sincere hope that other politicians and interest groups can put aside their partisan feelings, step back from their political agendas, and join with us in the search for the new directions which will lead us to a more stable and prosperous society.

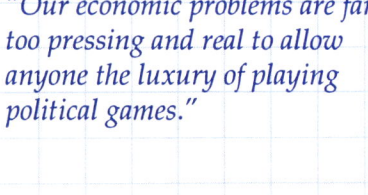

**Michael Harris, MPP**
**Leader, Progressive Conservative Party of Ontario**

*New Directions - A Blueprint for Economic Renewal & Prosperity*

# The Challenge

On September 23, 1991, the Premier of Ontario opened the fall session of the Legislature, and launched his government's second year in office, with these words:

*"It is now clear that Ontario faces its most serious economic challenge since the Great Depression. Unemployment is far too high. We have lost thousands of permanent jobs. Rural Ontario is in difficulty due to the collapse of farm incomes. Nearly a million Ontarians are relying on some kind of social assistance. Unemployment insurance is less effective than it needs to be. There is less trust and good will than there needs to be to build the basis for recovery."*

**Mike Harris agrees.**

Ontario is in recession. Economists define a recession as two consecutive quarters of decline in real gross national product. But this is a hard, dry and even inhuman definition. The human side is far more telling: the parents who can't pay the mortgage, and lose their home; the steelworker who is laid off after 20 years on the job, and can't balance the family budget; the entrepreneur who uses her life savings to start a small business, and sees it die from poor sales. For the victims, such losses often go hand in hand with a more intangible, but equally real, human loss of pride, spirit and hope.†

How has this happened in a province that has traditionally driven the Canadian economy - that provides 40% of our nation's jobs, and more than half its manufacturing capability?

The problem is that government - at all levels, and of all political stripes - has been over-spending, over-taxing, and over-simplistic in its approach to public policy, for far too long. Sound, long term, and seriously overdue fiscal, social and economic planning has been sacrificed for political expediency. And successive governments have left tremendous fiscal, social and economic debts for future generations to pay.

† Mike Harris, *'Ontario can beat the recession'*, The Financial Post, January 31, 1991

*"...Ontario faces its most serious economic challenge since the Great Depression."*

*"The problem is that government...has been over-spending, over-taxing, and over-simplistic..."*

 *New Directions - A Blueprint for Economic Renewal & Prosperity*

Three elections, four Premiers, and five governments since 1985 have generated no less than 50 tax increases in Ontario - with the biggest between 1987 and 1990. Since 1985, the provincial debt has risen dramatically, from $30 billion to $50 billion by April of 1992 - and is projected to almost double again to $100 billion in the next five years. Government spending and tax revenues have *more* than doubled since 1985.

In 1985, Ontario had a 10% competitive tax advantage over Quebec. The Conference Board of Canada rated us as very competitive against Japan, Europe, and most provinces and U.S. states. The Board's latest study (September 1991) finds that edge has disappeared. Today, Ontario is the highest taxed jurisdiction in all of North America and no longer enjoys any tax advantage.

Mike Harris has argued for years - before, during and after elections - that there's an urgent need to set priorities, focus on essentials, manage better, and plan for the future, and that government cannot continue to tax, spend and borrow like there's no tomorrow.

Well, it's tomorrow. By failing to acknowledge global trends toward more prudent fiscal agendas, or policies embraced by other jurisdictions to heighten competitiveness, many of Ontario's blessings are now at risk. The soaring cost of universal health care, welfare and social programs - along with massive ad hoc government intervention in the marketplace - have dangerously added to the cost of doing business, dampened investment, and severely crippled our ability to compete.

No society can enjoy the benefits of economic and social prosperity - whether it's well-paying jobs, decent housing, quality health care, excellence in education, good roads or a clean environment - unless it first has an economy capable of generating the wealth to sustain them.

In today's global economy, Ontario's prospects for renewal and prosperity depend entirely on our ability to compete. There is no choice. If we can't compete, we lose markets. Without markets, we lose jobs. And when we lose jobs, society experiences much more than social and economic loss. We suffer the most tragic of *human* losses...the loss of hope.

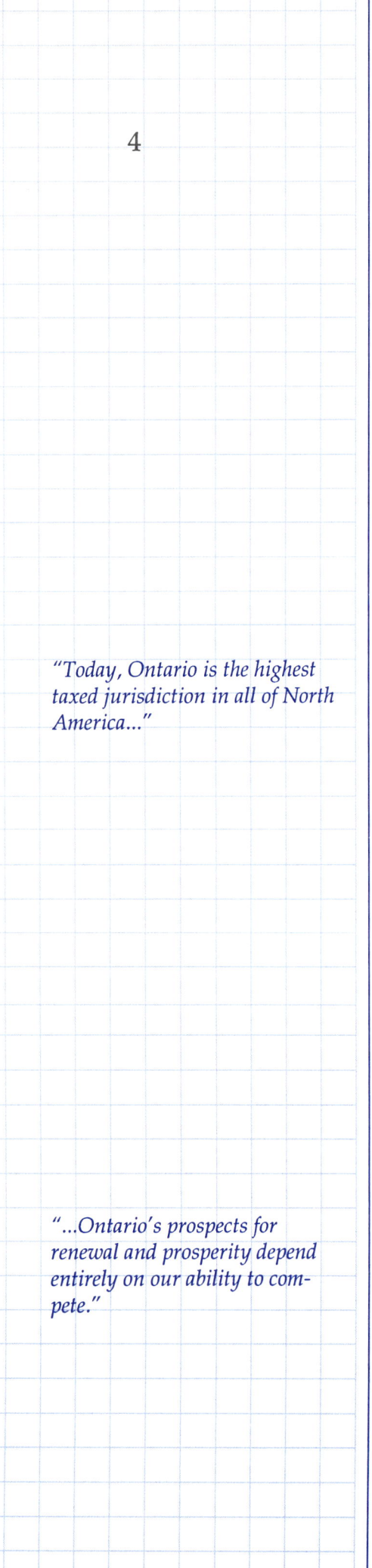

*"Today, Ontario is the highest taxed jurisdiction in all of North America..."*

*"...Ontario's prospects for renewal and prosperity depend entirely on our ability to compete."*

 *New Directions - A Blueprint for Economic Renewal & Prosperity*

On September 23rd, the Premier of Ontario observed:

*"These crises... point out several truths:*

*"Our industries have to be able to buy and sell in Canadian and world markets at competitive prices, or they will not be able to survive;*

*"Canadian workers are willing to make sacrifices when they know they're being treated fairly;*

*"Investment capital must be innovative and timely and look to the long term;*

*'And the organization of government must be mobilized more creatively to deal with the challenge of economic renewal in many different sectors of the economy."*

**Mike Harris agrees.**

And offers New Directions - A Blueprint for Economic Renewal & Prosperity in Ontario.

**Queen's Park
October 31, 1991**

# The Agenda

To develop comprehensive economic strategies to address critical public policy deficiencies with respect to jobs, training and investment.

## Highlights

❑ creation of a new Ontario Jobs, Adjustment & Training Secretariat

❑ wage subsidies for employers to link social assistance directly to jobs

❑ a moratorium on increases to the minimum wage

❑ choice of store openings with guaranteed protection for workers

❑ a moratorium on changes to the Labour Relations Act

❑ establishment of Industrial & Community Development Bond financing

❑ strategy to develop, use & market leading edge environmental technology

❑ immediate financial support for Ontario's agricultural community

❑ major and selected tax cuts, including a 1% reduction in provincial sales tax

❑ phase out of the Employer Health Levy (payroll tax) for small businesses

❑ expenditure controls to cut and re-direct government spending

❑ balanced budget requirement

❑ reformation of the budget consultation process

*New Directions - A Blueprint for Economic Renewal & Prosperity*

"As you noted in your December 4, 1990 statement on 'dealing with the recession and preparing for recovery', the Ontario economy entered into recession in April last year, with unemployment having since risen to over 7%. Job losses have been most pronounced in the manufacturing sector, where employment has fallen by 77,000 over the past year. Virtually all of this was attributed in that statement to the impact of federal interest rate and high dollar policies, free trade and the Goods and Services Tax. Each of these factors may have contributed in some way to the present downturn. But to singularly blame them for the current recession ignores a number of much deeper competitiveness problems at the provincial level."

**The Board of Trade of Metropolitan Toronto
Pre-budget Submission to the
Treasurer of Ontario
February 1991**

"The government of this province says it had to spend more to help those most affected by the recession. I won't quibble with that. We do, after all, have a responsibility to look after the disadvantaged and the less fortunate in our society. But I do find fault with the fact that despite being faced with an increase in spending of 13.5% and a decline in revenues of $435 million, the government couldn't find any areas worth cutting... and significantly costly programs that - since we can't afford them anyway - we could learn to live without. The government never asked the critical question of today. And that is: What are we going to abandon so we'll have the money to engage in these new or improved programs?"

**Lawrence G. Tapp
Lawson Mardon Group
Debt, Deficits & Taxes: Why We Can't Compete
Mike Harris Public Hearings on the Ontario Budget, May, 1991**

"The Ontario government does not seem to understand you cannot spend yourself rich. There is no free lunch and the additional costs to carry the deficit will eventually result in higher overall costs and further erode the ability of Ontario manufacturers to compete on a global scale. The creation of a solid investment climate should have been the top priority to retain and increase jobs in Ontario. Price stability cannot be reached without provincial cooperation, this includes a better fiscal policy, more stable wage policy, sales tax harmonization and removal of regulated pricing restraints."

**Canadian Manufacturer's Association
Mike Harris Public Hearings on the Ontario Budget, May 15, 1991**

*"...despite...an increase in spending of 13.5% and a decline in revenues of $435 million, the government couldn't find any areas worth cutting..."*

# JOBS, TRAINING & INVESTMENT

### Job Creation, Adjustment & Training Strategies

Let's start with the basics. There is an urgent need for job creation, adjustment and training strategies in Ontario. At least one million Ontarians are now receiving social assistance - at a cost that may well surpass $5 billion by 1991/92. The number of people whose Unemployment Insurance has run out is up to nearly 40,000 per month - with more than 10% likely to require social assistance. The vast majority are ready, willing, and able to work, or to be retrained.

### ❏ Ontario Jobs, Adjustment & Training Secretariat

A new Secretariat is needed to develop job, adjustment and training strategies. It should have a mandate to link the provision of social assistance benefits directly to employment, skills development, adjustment, training, retraining, apprenticeship and education. The secretariat would be responsible *only* for establishing priorities and policy. Programs would then be delivered by the appropriate Ministries.

The Ontario Jobs, Adjustment & Training Secretariat would be funded by streamlining, downsizing and eventually phasing out the Ministry of Skills Development. Much of its $265 million budget is now being spent on administration, duplication and bureaucracy. Transferring policy-setting to the Secretariat, and programs to more appropriate Ministries or delivery agencies, would improve decision-making, and free up millions of dollars for training programs, tax initiatives and new priorities.

*"Ontario's manufacturing continues to go through deep changes. So are all sectors of the economy: services, retail, the financial sector. I have to tell the House that while there are some signs of a modest recovery in parts of our economy, major changes in our core manufacturing base are still happening. The layoffs are not over."*

**Premier Bob Rae**
**Statement to the Ontario Legislature**
**September 23, 1991**

*"At least one million Ontarians are now receiving social assistance."*

*"The...Secretariat would be funded by streamlining, downsizing, and eventually phasing out the Ministry of Skills Development."*

*New Directions - A Blueprint for Economic Renewal & Prosperity*

❏ **Job Creation**

A job creation strategy should include, but not be limited to:

❏ **wage subsidies to employers hiring social assistance recipients**

Thousands of Ontarians now on social assistance are able to work, yet employers cannot afford to hire them. By linking social assistance directly to employment, as recommended in the SARC report, Queen's Park could effectively create a multi-billion dollar pool of money - topped up by employers - to put people back to work, at *no extra cost to taxpayers*. Each new job, in fact, would boost government revenues without tax hikes. Those added revenues could then be used for targeted tax relief.

*"...Queen's Park could effectively create a multi-billion dollar pool of money... to put people back to work, at no extra cost to taxpayers."*

❏ **targeted tax relief in the small business, tourist and retail sectors**

Targeted tax relief in the small business, tourist and retail sectors would create jobs, benefit consumers and restore business confidence. Tax *'holidays'*, or one time exemptions for targeted sectors or products, can help stimulate growth reviving both consumer interest and employment. The targets and amount of relief would vary depending on which industry or sector was in trouble. Any government revenue loss would be offset by spending controls and economic growth.

❏ **increased day care funding to facilitate workplace entry/re-entry**

Increased day care funding should be targeted directly at parents, and on the basis of need, to create more opportunities to access the workplace. By encouraging regulated private sector involvement in the creation of day care spaces, and by subsidizing needy families, parents could be assured of both choice and quality care.

❏ **moratorium on legislated minimum wage increases**

A University of Toronto study found 53,000 jobs would be lost if the NDP keeps its promise to hike the minimum wage to 60% of the average industrial wage over five years. Ontario cannot afford to lose another 53,000 jobs. Higher wages for workers should be the result of a strong and competitive economic climate, not of political philosophy.

*"Ontario cannot afford to lose another 53,000 jobs."*

## ❏ Job Creation continued

### ❏ Sunday shopping

Both the existing Liberal legislation, and the proposed NDP laws, are unfair, unworkable and bad for Ontario's economic well-being.

Sunday openings and shopping should be self-regulated. Let business compete and create jobs in the process. Full-time employees who do not wish to work on Sunday or any other day of their choice should be protected with an enforceable, legislated right to a family pause day. However, those who wish for or need employment on Sundays should be given a chance to work.

*"Sunday openings and shopping should be self-regulated."*

*New Directions - A Blueprint for Economic Renewal & Prosperity*

## ❑ Adjustment & Training

The Canadian Federation of Independent Business reports that 59 percent of its Ontario members face a significant problem in finding skilled workers. We believe that every young person in Ontario should have a marketable skill along with a well-rounded education. A skilled and educated workforce is a primary component of economic competitiveness, and producing such a workforce must be a priority for our educational system.

The questions of educational reform will be dealt with in detail in a future New Directions paper, but we believe the following steps should be taken now...

### ❑ Skilled labour

While core academic skills must be maintained and accountability must rest with the government, there is room for private sector involvement in the learning process. Using education and social welfare funding, on the job training should be incorporated in both the educational and training/re-training systems.

The Ontario Jobs, Adjustment and Training Secretariat would play a role in consultation, and by cooperating, with its social, labour and business partners to determine the necessary priorities for new and existing programs.

### ❑ Apprenticeship

Ontario's antiquated and ineffective apprenticeship system needs to be overhauled to make it more accessible, and to shorten the lengthy training periods. Curriculum must address current technology, legislation must be updated to allow higher renumeration, and the institutional barriers which discourage young people from entering apprenticeship must be removed.

### ❑ Centres of specialization

The modern job marketplace demands a higher degree of specialized knowledge and skills than ever before. While Ontario's community colleges do an excellent job of teaching and training students, and should continue in that role, a select number of community colleges should also be allowed to concentrate their resources and become centres of specialization. They would provide state-of-the-art training for technological specialties to address our future needs, and share those specialized resources with other post-secondary institutions.

*"We believe that every young person in Ontario should have a marketable skill along with a well-rounded education."*

*"...a select number of community colleges should...become centres of specialization."*

*New Directions - A Blueprint for Economic Renewal & Prosperity*

## Investment Strategy

Ontario's shrinking ability to retain or attract investment is reaching crisis proportions. Ongoing concern about the government's ability to manage the economy - a perception that the voice of business is not heeded at Queen's Park - an unprecedented $10 billion deficit - and proposed reforms to the Labour Relations Act - have all discouraged investor confidence.

Every sector of the economy has been affected. Small businesses, manufacturing, construction, financial, and resource-based companies are all being hurt by the economic downturn, and many are cancelling investment plans as a result of the political uncertainty at Queen's Park.

Business wants to invest. But many companies are responding to retro-active legislation, mixed signals and economically detrimental public policy here in Ontario by looking to other jurisdictions for investment opportunities. Interest from the out-of-province investment community has all but dried up.

Ontario needs investment to grow and prosper. And government has a responsibility to provide sound, balanced economic leadership, planning and creative opportunities to attract this investment.

*"Interest from the out-of-province investment community has all but dried up."*

"The survey has shown that since the Ontario budget came down, 63 per cent of small businesses in the province have decreased their hiring plans, while another 57 per cent have cut their capital investment spending. Furthermore, she added, nearly four out of five small businesses - 77 per cent - are highly concerned about the Ontario government's plan to make union organizing easier within business. Smaller firms in the construction industry, at 86 per cent, along with manufacturing, at 84 per cent, have the greatest concern in this regard."

'Survey finds one-third of the small business sector in Ontario - 36% - report they are considering moving all or part of their operations out of the province -putting 500,000 jobs at risk.'

**News Release**
**Canadian Federation Independent Business**
**October 3, 1991**

### ❑ Hospitable Business Climate

In a battle between the business community and the government of the day there can be no winner, and the economy of Ontario is the only sure loser. A renewed attempt must be made to provide substantive and responsive consultation on economic and fiscal policies. Only an open and meaningful two-way dialogue can restore business confidence, provide useful input for policy-makers, and remove the uncertainty investors feel about the potential policy directions of government.

*"Only an open and meaningful two-way dialogue can restore business confidence..."*

A mechanism for encouraging balanced input in the overall fiscal direction of government is described under "Reforming the Budgetary Process" on page 30.

### ❑ Moratorium on Labour Law Changes

A survey conducted by Ernst and Young for the All Business Coalition found the business community believes the new labour laws under consideration by the NDP would cost Ontario up to 480,000 jobs. That is one-fourth of all the jobs in the province. As well, the study indicated that up to $20 billion in future investment over the next five years is in jeopardy if the proposed changes are enacted.

*"...the business community believes the new labour laws under consideration by the NDP would cost Ontario up to 480 thousand jobs."*

Until a process of legitimate consultation is established (as described under "Hospitable Business Climate" above), and until there is time for policy direction to be re-examined in light of the input of business and interest groups, there should be a moratorium on changes to the Labour Relations Act.

 *New Directions - A Blueprint for Economic Renewal & Prosperity*

## ❏ Industrial Development Bonds

Ontario needs creative solutions to generate new investment, and especially to support economic diversification in rural and regional communities. Development bonds - 100% guaranteed by government - have proven to be an excellent vehicle in other jurisdictions to attract investment in order to create long term employment opportunities. IDBs help people create their own jobs right at home.

Interested communities would establish Bond Corporations (with government approval), and raise money for equity investments from local residents as well as institutional investors. The investments would be locked in for a minimum of two years, at which time investors could choose to cash them in for their principal value, convert them into stock in the company or companies involved, or roll them over into another long-term investment in the Bond Corporation.

## ❏ Community Development Bonds

In the same vein, Community Development Bonds may well be an ideal way to get major infrastructure projects funded. The Ontario Home Builders' Association proposed a similar investment option more than a year ago. This kind of bond financing, similar to savings bonds, would assist communities to spread costs more evenly over time, and let those who benefit pay equally.

Public interest could be stimulated by exempting earned interest on the bonds from taxation. Such bonds - safe, secure, and tax-free - would attract considerable institutional investment, including pension funds.

*"IDB's help people create their own jobs right at home."*

*"Such bonds...would attract considerable institutional investment, including pension funds."*

*New Directions - A Blueprint for Economic Renewal & Prosperity*

Building on the OHBA model, Queen's Park, with assistance from the federal government, could establish a Provincial Funding Corporation to underwrite or guarantee both Industrial and Community Development Bonds. Tax law changes could be implemented to deal with interest income for investors and reduce debt costs. This whole concept deserves consideration in the April 1992 budget.

*\* Note: pension funds, and worker ownership, as investment vehicle: There is evidence the current government intends to proceed on two related fronts: a Pension Based Investment Fund, and an Ontario Investment and Worker ownership program.*

*Examples at Spruce Falls and Algoma indicate worker ownership and related government-sponsored investment as envisioned by the current government is unrelated to technological development. Further, both approaches involve costly bureaucracy, and are subject to political dictates. The Development Bond approach would facilitate objectives of both worker ownership and public sector pension-based investment - at less cost, and with better results. With Development Bonds, both workers and pension fund managers would be able to invest - but, unlike proposals to establish formal mechanisms to induce investment - only on the basis of sound market investment considerations.*

 *New Directions - A Blueprint for Economic Renewal & Prosperity*

### ❑ Ontario Hydro Reforms

Ontario once enjoyed energy costs that were among the lowest in all of North America. That was good for consumers as well as for business. But Ontario's reputation as a source of affordable, dependable energy is no longer a selling card. Today, homeowners pay one-third more than people in other provinces, large industries pay two-thirds more, and everyone faces a 44% hike over the next three years.

Industry must have a reliable and affordable energy source. Without it, Ontario cannot expect to attract new investment in the industrial sector, and faces the potential loss of more businesses to other jurisdictions.

While people continue to debate the merits and cost of nuclear power, it's clear Ontario Hydro can and must cut costs. The most logical place to start is with the overhead.

According to Energy Probe, Ontario Hydro's 33,000 person payroll - which accounts for one-third of our electricity bills - "is bloated almost beyond belief." The average salary is an astonishing $65,000 a year. Utilities in the rest of the country, it says, average 24% fewer employees to produce the same amount of power.

Consumers and the environment would benefit if Ontario Hydro privatized more generating stations and opened up the electricity sector to competition. Hydro should also expand the opportunities for co-generation and continue to purchase power at the same price at which the utility produces it.

We are also deeply concerned by the current trend towards using Ontario Hydro as a tool for social engineering, instead of in its traditional role as a supplier of safe and economical electricity to the Ontario economy.

*"But that is just one aspect of the problem. In the next decade, Hydro will spend $6 billion - an average of $166 a bill-payer a year - on a grab bag of uneconomic conservation programs. Many of them will pay people to buy products they would have purchased anyway; many, such as a program to encourage heat pump air conditioners, will increase electrical consumption."*

**Lawrence Solomon**<br>**Energy Probe**<br>**Globe and Mail, October 4, 1991**

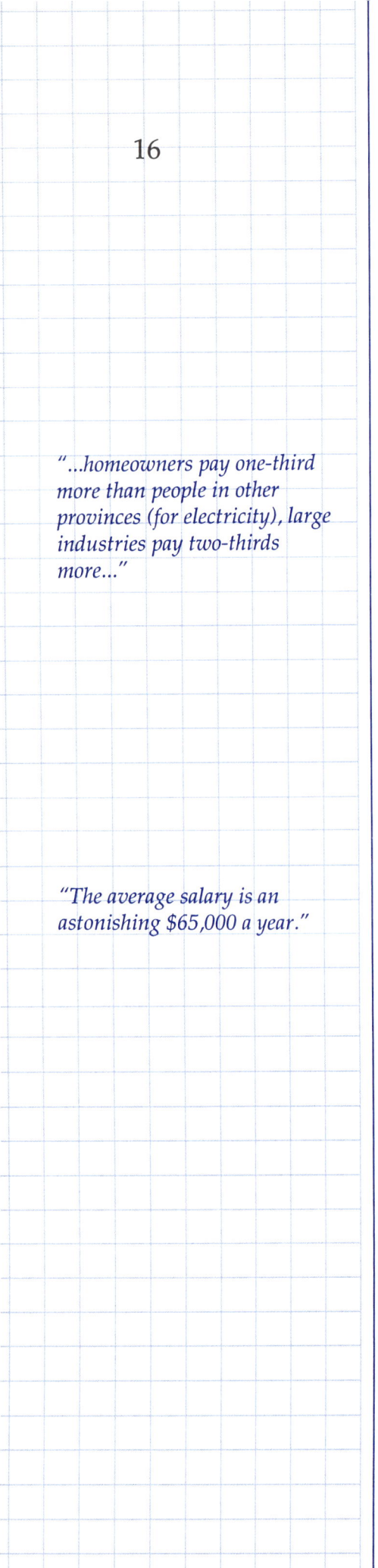

*"...homeowners pay one-third more than people in other provinces (for electricity), large industries pay two-thirds more..."*

*"The average salary is an astonishing $65,000 a year."*

## ❏ Environmental Technology

The global environmental challenge presents global economic opportunities for Ontario.

Mike Harris has developed a billion dollar economic strategy to spark the development, use and world-wide marketing of leading edge environmental technology. All of the funding required to implement this strategy already exists within Ontario government coffers, existing industrial support programs, and regional grants and loans. No new revenues are required.

The plan, dubbed BEST (Best Environmental Support and Technology), would be anchored by a $330 million investment - from the unallocated balance in the Ontario Technology Fund - over seven years, to assist Ontario companies to research, build and sell new environmental technology.

As part of this province-wide strategy, an environmental support and technology focus would also be given to other government grant, loan or regional development programs.

Environmentalists, industrialists, universities, colleges and research agencies - along with other private and public sector stakeholders - would be involved in developing and implementing the strategy. The Ontario government would assume a leadership role, and mobilize its resources.

The objective would be the creation of a multi-billion dollar industry in Ontario - a clean, viable and value-added industry - that would bring proven environmental technology on stream for application in both domestic and foreign markets. That's good for jobs, *and* the environment.

It would go hand in hand with the urgent need in this province to modernize, restructure, and create new opportunities for Ontario's core manufacturing and resource-based industries.

*"All of the funding required to implement this strategy already exists...No new revenues are required."*

*New Directions - A Blueprint for Economic Renewal & Prosperity*

*"If Ontario can develop a process to clean up the Great Lakes, we can export that technology to clean up the world's lakes. If we can develop the technology to clean up our own garbage crisis, we can share that knowledge to solve the world's garbage crisis. If we can lead the rest of the world in the development of any new environmental technology, for that matter, the rest of the world will beat a path to our door to buy it. And by applying the best available environmental technology here in Ontario, we can sustain our forestry, mining and resource industries; we can bring more housing and industrial development on stream faster, cheaper and safer; we can create jobs and opportunities for a whole new generation of Ontarians; and we can be proud of the fact that we did it responsibly."*

**Mike Harris**
**Leader**
**Ontario PC Party**
**Campaign '90**

### ❏ Housing and Construction Industry Stimulation

The current system of rent control legislation fails to provide any incentives for the construction of new rental accommodation, and has also proven inadequate for protection of tenant interests.

*"The current system...fails to provide any incentives...and has also proven inadequate for protection of tenant interests."*

Direct subsidy of renters, rather than buildings, would save the government the massive costs of construction, stimulate new investment and employment in the sector, and improve tenant's ability to find adequate and affordable housing.

The province should also streamline its approval process for new housing initiatives, and encourage municipalities to do the same.

The larger questions of government's role in the housing sector will be dealt with in a future New Directions paper.

*New Directions - A Blueprint for Economic Renewal & Prosperity*

## ❏ Support for Ontario's Agricultural Community

Ontario's agriculture sector is experiencing the bleakest conditions it has ever known. Debt loads are mounting for thousands of producers; the search for off-farm employment grows, made even more difficult in a recession-afflicted economy; retirement reserves and other forms of life savings are cashed in a desperate attempt to pay crop bills and secure family needs; other bills go unpaid; participation in debt review hearings grows; and bit by bit, family farms, sometimes those which have been in the family for more than a century, are sold off to speculators, or to those seeking country estates, as a means of staving off formal bankruptcy. This is what farmers are going through, and government must respond.

The agricultural crisis is the result of an international trade war. Ontario farm efficiency is among the highest in the world, but Ontario support levels are substantially lower than in other developed countries of the world - and lower than in other Canadian provinces.

Ontario's 60,000 farm families will not survive unless government steps in. It will cost about $124 million to remain competitive in the face of skyrocketing subsidization in other jurisdictions. But it's worth every dime. Rather than bailing out failed and obsolete industries at a cost of *many* hundreds of millions of dollars, as the Ontario government is doing today, this money would be better spent by investing in the long term future of Ontario's all important farm community.

The price is a low one when you consider that government would avoid the high price of reduced property taxes, increased welfare payments, and other associated costs of bankrupt farm families, as well as land stewardship costs associated with vacant or abandoned farm properties.

The long-term solution can only come from success at GATT and other international and national forums in eliminating subsidies. Once a level, subsidy-free playing field is achieved, prices will rise and subsidies can be reduced. In the meantime, government must do what it can to reduce foreign and competing domestic price advantages and enable Ontario's farm families to survive.

*"Ontario's 60,000 farm families will not survive unless government steps in."*

*"...government would avoid...reduced property taxes, increased welfare payments, and other...costs of bankrupt farm families..."*

 *New Directions - A Blueprint for Economic Renewal & Prosperity*

Such actions should not only include subsidies, but the following initiatives:

❏ Continued research to support import replacement and market development

❏ A long-term program for soil conservation

❏ Encouraging the development of benign agricultural technology

❏ Incentives for the development and use of blended ethanol gasoline

❏ Agricultural research and development under the "BEST" program

### 'Open Letter to Bob Rae - August 21, 1991'

*"It is critical for your government to decide whether it really wants to maintain a viable family farm agriculture in this province, for indeed, almost all Ontario farms are family owned and operated. No self-esteemed corporation would tolerate the low prices and high risks which characterize 1991 agriculture. It is critical for you and the government of Ontario to decide whether it is important to support farm-based rural communities and whether Ontario citizens should eat Ontario-grown food."*

**Roger George**
President
Ont. Fed. of Agriculture

**Larry Meihls**
Chair
Ont. Soybean Growers' Marketing Board

**Frank Anthony**
President
Ont. Corn Producers' Ass.

**George Demtriuc**
Chair
Ont. Wheat Producers' Marketing Board

*New Directions - A Blueprint for Economic Renewal & Prosperity*

## ❏ Rural and Regional Development Strategies

The development bond concept has tremendous potential for application as part of rural and regional development strategies - a powerful tool to facilitate community and industrial development. But the Ontario government must provide better leadership and mechanisms to find long term solutions.

## ❏ Northern Development Directorate

One such model may be the Northern Development Directorate first proposed by Mike Harris during the 1990 election - an organization of volunteer native, business, municipal and labour representatives, with a mandate to identify, co-ordinate, and recommend approaches to address northern development priorities and opportunities - including tourism, transportation, health care, education, and economic diversification.

Various levels of government currently spend more than a billion dollars each year on various economic and social development initiatives in Northern Ontario. Yet, many Northerners feel shut out of the decision-making and priority setting process. A Northern Development Directorate allows those who are affected by the decisions made at Queen's Park to set priorities, and to make the right decisions.

*"...many Northerners feel shut out of the decision-making and priority-setting process."*

 *New Directions - A Blueprint for Economic Renewal & Prosperity*

# FISCAL & BUDGETARY POLICIES

Hard times require hard decisions, and the fiscal and budgetary policies of a government must come under even closer scrutiny to ensure they are responsible to *both* the economic and social needs of the taxpayer.

As the tax base shrinks, the temptation grows to increase the tax rates and impose new taxes to keep revenues steady. However, this succeeds only in reducing business competitiveness as well as the incentive to expand and invest.

The answer is to expand the tax base again by giving business the opportunity to grow and create jobs, and giving consumers the incentive to purchase more goods and services.

## Taxation

Ontario is now the most heavily taxed jurisdiction in all of North America. A number of major tax cuts and reforms are required to stimulate economic activity and enhance competitiveness.

### ❑ Provincial Sales Tax

Ontario's provincial sales tax should be reduced by a full one percentage point - from the current 8% to 7%. This major tax cut should be implemented immediately to recapture consumer and retail business confidence, and to help reduce one of the major incentives for cross-border shopping. The entire provincial economy would benefit.

The full-year cost of this move would reduce government revenues by approximately $1 billion - which would be partially offset by new tax revenues being generated through increased employment and economic activity. Public sector expenditure controls (see pages 25 - 29) would make up the balance.

*"...the temptation grows (for government) to increase the tax rates and impose new taxes...The answer is to expand the tax base again..."*

*"Ontario's provincial sales tax should be reduced by a full percentage point - from the current 8% to 7%."*

*New Directions - A Blueprint for Economic Renewal & Prosperity*

## ❏ Gasoline and Fuel Tax

Gasoline and fuel taxes should be immediately cut by 10%. This would benefit all sectors of the economy, including transportation, tourism and manufacturing. Combined with a reduction in PST, these cuts would begin to address ongoing concerns and job losses associated with cross-border shopping.

The full year cost of a 10% gasoline tax cut would be approximately $160 million. For fuel taxes, it would be $37 million. Again, both costs are in the form of foregone revenues to government; and can be fully offset by new revenues generated by economic activity, along with expenditure controls.

## ❏ Employer Health Levy (Payroll Taxes)

The Employer Health Levy is a hidden tax, tied directly to payrolls. It's a tax on jobs, a tax on higher wages, and a tax on consumers by adding to the cost of goods and services. It has also been a major factor in eroding the ability of Ontario companies to compete with other jurisdictions and provinces.

The Employer Health Levy should be phased out over a two year period for all companies with payrolls of less than $400,000. This would exempt the small business sector, which has been responsible for the majority of job creation in Ontario in recent years. A two-year phase-out would allow Queen's Park to adjust it's spending policies to accommodate the reduction in revenue, estimated at $325 million.*

Again, some of the lost revenues would be partially offset by increased economic activity. But we believe government should fully facilitate this initiative through spending controls. According to the current budgetary projections, overall provincial spending will be $56.1 billion and $60.3 billion over the next two years respectively. With a two-year phase out of the payroll tax for small business, that means Queen's Park would be required to cut spending by less than 0.6% in the first year, and little more than 0.5% the next.

---

\* Based on extrapolations from current EHT revenues and original full-year tax bracket yield estimate from Ministry of Treasury and Economics, Tax Policy Branch.

> *"Gasoline and fuel taxes should be immediately cut by 10%."*

> *"The Employer Health Levy should be phased out over a two year period for all companies with payrolls of less than $400,000."*

*"Government estimates (of lost revenue) have ranged...to $300 million."*

❑ **Collect PST at the border**

Failure to collect legally due PST at the border puts a greater burden on the Ontario taxpayers.

There is currently no reliable estimate of the potential revenue impact of this measure. If the estimated total of $2.2 billion in sales the province looses annually to cross-border shopping was on taxable transactions, the lost revenue cost would be about $176 million.

Government estimates have ranged higher, from $140 million to $300 million.

*"The London Chamber of Commerce believes that the recent NDP budget is perhaps the most irresponsible budget in the history of Ontario. The projected $9.7 billion deficit in fiscal '92, when combined with projected sizeable deficits in the following fiscal years, adds up to financial chaos for our province... Certainly the lesson learned by the Federal government in the early 1970s and 1980s should be heeded. It is well known that governments which attempt to spend their way out of recessions simply leave a debt-ridden legacy. This government is demonstrating that they have little or no understanding of the emerging one world marketplace and the need for Ontario to be competitive. This budget is accelerating the perception in international circles that Ontario is a poor place to conduct business."*

**Bryan Thomas**
**Chairman of the Board**
**London Chamber of Commerce**
**Submission to Mike Harris Task Force on the Budget**
**June 4, 1991**

*"Harris said he would not promise to match the Quebec program, Outaouais, which can offer attractive grants, loans and tax holidays to high-technology companies. He said lower taxes are the best way to make the Ontario economy attractive to businesses and he can't do that if he increases spending."*

**Ottawa Citizen**
**August 23, 1990**

*New Directions - A Blueprint for Economic Renewal & Prosperity*

## **Spending Controls**

The proposed tax measures would have an immediate effect of reducing Ontario government revenues by approximately $1.5 billion dollars annually. The economic measures contained in this document to stimulate investment, economic activity and job creation will generate new tax revenues to substantially offset this revenue loss. Up to $300 million more would be recovered in the collection of PST at the border. But in view of the unacceptable budgetary deficit this year - and those proposed over the next four years - serious, meaningful expenditure control must be a priority.

### ❑ Public Sector Restraint

Without any program cuts, there are many millions of dollars in government spending that could be saved by eliminating administrative waste and duplication. Cutting down on consultants, administrative costs, office space, travel and hotel bookings is not only possible, but necessary.

The size of the public service should be reduced to 1985 levels through attrition and early retirement. Every one thousand middle management positions that are phased out will save the government $60 million in wages and benefits per year (i.e. 5,000 positions = $300 million).

There are also a number of redundant and unnecessary government programs that can, and should be, eliminated. We have already proposed the creation of an Expenditure Review Committee with a mandate to find non-productive programs that should be cut, and administrative re-alignments which could save taxpayers' money.

The budgetary system within the government bureaucracy must also be changed. Right now, senior bureaucrats are actually encouraged to waste public funds...a department must spend all of the money allocated it in a fiscal year in order to get full funding for the next year. This provides an incentive for wasteful spending, particularly towards the end of each fiscal year. Instead, departments should be allowed to roll over any additional funds into the next fiscal year. As well, performance bonuses for senior civil servants should be based on both results *and* savings.

The provisions of Conservative MPP David Tilson's private member's bill requiring disclosure of civil servant salaries and benefits would help lead to greater accountability and restraint.

---

*"...in view of the unacceptable budgetary deficit...serious, meaningful expenditure control must be a priority."*

*"The size of the public service should be reduced to 1985 levels through attrition and early retirement."*

*"...senior bureaucrats are actually encouraged to waste public funds..."*

*New Directions - A Blueprint for Economic Renewal & Prosperity*

*"...a requirement that when a new government program is created, a set date for termination of that program is included."*

❑ **Mandatory Sunset Review**

One way to assist this process is to legislate mandatory sunset review. A motion to do this has been tabled twice in the Ontario Legislature...by Mike Harris in 1989, and again in 1991 by Conservative MPP Gary Carr. A sunset clause is a requirement that when a new government program is created, a set date for termination of that program is included. Prior to that date, the program is reviewed and subsequently changed, continued or terminated.

In the case of existing programs, mandatory evaluations would be initiated to justify or streamline the programs continued operation.

❑ **Public Sector Wages**

Ontario's public service is among the best in North America. Public servants also enjoy among the highest wages, the best pension plans, the greatest job security and tremendous employment benefits.

*"...$24 billion is used for salaries and benefits for government employees, and others...in the broader public service."*

Forty-five percent of the provincial budget - $24 billion - is used for salaries and benefits for government employees, and others such as teachers, hospital workers and municipal workers in the broader public service. Each 1% average increase in combined Ontario public service and broader public service wages costs provincial taxpayers $240 million. This year, the settlement was 5.8%. Some senior managers received bonuses of up to $11,000 per year. When you factor in benefits, pay equity, merit increases, and special bonuses, the total public sector compensation package went up by more than 16%.

Lower wage settlements would fully offset the entire $1 billion cost of reducing the PST by one percentage point. As long as the economic downturn continues - with millions in the private sector who are now jobless and on welfare - Queen's Park should adopt a policy to link public sector settlements in support of tax reductions, and base settlements on new revenue generated by new economic activity.

On this basis, settlements for the Ontario public service could be expected come in somewhere between 0% and 3%.

*New Directions - A Blueprint for Economic Renewal & Prosperity*

### ❏ Balanced Budget

A balanced budget requirement would force government to control spending, limit borrowing, and focus on spending priorities. There is no such requirement at the provincial level in Ontario today, although municipalities and school boards are bound by legislation to balance their budgets.

Mike Harris has tabled private member's Bill 138 calling for the creation of a balanced budget requirement at the provincial level - perhaps every three to five years. If a government could not balance its budget, or felt it had good reason to go into debt on the public's behalf, it would have to call either a referendum on its economic plan, or a general election.

Harris suggests putting a balanced budget question on a municipal ballot to give the Ontario electorate an opportunity to make its views known. If there was sufficient support, work could begin on designing a balanced budget law with the input of the public, labour, business, and all political parties.

Unfortunately, the size of the current deficit and the lingering recession make it impossible to balance today's budget with an immediate stroke of the pen. Instead, it will be necessary to first stop the growth in government spending and borrowing, cut unnecessary and wasteful expenditures, and put a priority on stimulating growth in investment and jobs.

Above all, it will require a new attitude on the part of government...a willingness to put fiscal responsibility at the top of the agenda. The decisions that must be made will not be easy, but the dangers of the downward debt/borrowing/taxation spiral must be recognized, and the political courage must be summoned to break that pattern while there is still time to do so.

There has to be a will before there can be a way.

*"...it will require a new attitude on the part of government...a willingness to put fiscal responsibility at the top of the agenda."*

### ❏ Health Care Reform

The largest and fastest-growing expenditure for the Ontario government is the maintenance of our health care system, arguably the finest in the world in terms of quality and accessibility.

Maintaining that quality without putting an unbearable economic load on taxpayers means careful analysis of the present system, and reforms aimed at ensuring the maximum possible efficiency.

Efficiency gains will be essential to maintain quality and accessibility while dealing with demographic shifts which will put upward pressure on health care costs. The aging of Ontario's population will require us to place a greater emphasis on, and to dedicate more resources to, long term care and the development of a humane, cost-effective, and non-institutional response to the health care needs of seniors.

These subjects will be dealt with in detail in an upcoming New Directions paper, but the size ($17 billion dollars in the 1991 fiscal year) and effect of the health care budget merit its inclusion here.

Controlling the size of that budget will require a shift in attitude among both health care providers and users. Accountability must be built into both sides of the system so that no-one can lose sight of the fact that health care costs are subsidized directly from the taxpayer's purse.

One direction that must be taken is toward more private sector involvement. The challenges of the increasing costs and complexity of modern health care cannot be met by government in isolation.

*"The aging of Ontario's population will require us to place a greater emphasis on...long term care..."*

*"Accountability must be built into both sides of the (health care) system..."*

*New Directions - A Blueprint for Economic Renewal & Prosperity*

## Other Policy Reforms

### ❑ Impact Analysis

Many government public policy decisions are initiated without any consideration as to how they impact on existing government-mandated costs on business. A competitive impact analysis on any government initiative should be mandatory, and subject to public review and comment.

New policies should also be analyzed to determine their economic impact and ensure they will have the desired effect when combined with other initiatives.

### ❑ Windfall Allocation

The fast-growing provincial debt creates a cash drain for the government, demanding that money better spent on programs for people be used to make interest payments. That is why debt reduction must be a top priority.

Any windfall from higher-than-expected revenue should be directly applied against the deficit each year.

If the province ever manages to pay off its debt, any in-year revenue windfalls should be directed into a "rainy day account" for use in future economic hard times or emergencies.

*"A competitive impact analysis on any government intitiative should be mandatory, and subject to public review and comment."*

*"Any windfall from higher-than-expected revenue should be directly applied against the deficit each year."*

 *New Directions - A Blueprint for Economic Renewal & Prosperity*

## Reforming the Budgetary Process

❑ **Pre-budget Consultation**

The economic decisions made by the Ontario government have a profound effect on the lives of everyone in the province. The prices of both necessities and luxuries, basic decisions as to what to buy, where to work, how to live, can all be decided to a large extent by the contents of a provincial budget.

Traditionally, those contents have been the subject of much speculation in the days and weeks before a budget presentation. Taxpayers, business leaders, and investors are kept on seat-edge, waiting to see what happens.

Even though there is some pre-budget consultation, no participant can be sure whether the government is going to act on the concerns and suggestions presented, and the government reveals little of its plans.

Much of this secrecy and tension is not necessary.

Obviously, there are some measures which must be kept secret until budget day to prevent information from being exploited for personal gain. However, there is no reason the public must be kept in the dark about economic forecasts, government priorities, and policy options.

Instead of a flurry of limited consultation before each budget, there should be regular, public meetings with business leaders and interest groups to reveal this information and discuss possible actions.

In this way, the taxpayers...upon whose behalf the government is raising, spending, and borrowing money...will understand the nature of the decisions being made and the reasoning behind them.

As well, a public, on-going consultative process should lead to a more responsive government with the benefit of fully-informed public input.

*"...there is no reason the public must be kept in the dark about economic forecasts, government priorities, and policy options."*

*New Directions - A Blueprint for Economic Renewal & Prosperity*

## ❑ Post-budget Consultation

Once a budget has been presented, an opportunity must be given for full and frank public reaction, *before* budget legislation is passed.

Full public hearings on the entire budgetary package should be mandatory, with all non-essential measures not to take effect until the tri-partite committee holding the hearings has filed its report.

In arranging any budgetary consultation, all three political parties should share equally in the responsibility and opportunity of inviting groups or individuals to attend. Only in this way can a truly representative and balanced selection of opinion and information be obtained.

*"Full public hearings on the entire budgetary package should be mandatory..."*

> *"...to open the doors to all sectors of the public and to fellow Members of the Legislature for discussion and debate..."*

# Conclusion

In presenting this first in a series of New Directions papers, our purpose has been two-fold.

First, to offer a realistic set of alternative policies that we believe would address the serious economic problems facing our province.

Second, to open the door to all sectors of the public and to fellow Members of the Legislature for discussion and debate on our ideas and any other new proposals.

We stand ready, not only to explain the blueprint we have set out in this paper, but to listen to any and all reasoned voices that may contribute to reaching our common goal of improving the lives of all Ontarians.

**Members of the Caucus**
**Progressive Conservative Party of Ontario**

*We welcome your comments, suggestions, and criticisms regarding the policies outlined in this document. Please address your correspondence to the Office of the Leader, or to the appropriate critic.*

| Portfolios | Name | Address |
|---|---|---|
| Leader | Michael Harris | Room 116<br>Legislative Building<br>Queen's Park, Toronto<br>Ontario, M7A-1A8 |
| Northern Development,<br>Intergov'tal Affairs,<br>Constitutional Affairs | Ernie Eves | Room 167<br>Legislative Building<br>Queen's Park, Toronto<br>Ontario, M7A-1A8 |
| Education,<br>Skills Development,<br>Colleges and Universities | Dianne Cunningham | Room 172<br>Legislative Building<br>Queen's Park, Toronto<br>Ontario, M7A-1A8 |
| Treasury and Economics,<br>Revenue | Norm Sterling | Room 160<br>Legislative Building<br>Queen's Park, Toronto<br>Ontario, M7A-1A8 |
| Small Business,<br>Tourism and Recreation | Ted Arnott | Room 108 NW<br>Legislative Building<br>Queen's Park, Toronto<br>Ontario, M7A-1A8 |
| Industry, Trade and<br>Technology | Gary Carr | Room 107 NW<br>Legislative Building<br>Queen's Park, Toronto<br>Ontario, M7A-1A8 |

### New Directions - A Blueprint for Economic Renewal & Prosperity

| Portfolios | Name | Address |
|---|---|---|
| Environment, Citizenship, Race Relations, Human Rights | Don Cousens | Room 153<br>Legislative Building<br>Queen's Park, Toronto<br>Ontario, M7A-1A8 |
| Attorney-General, Native Affairs | Charles Harnick | Room 157<br>Legislative Building<br>Queen's Park, Toronto<br>Ontario, M7A-1A8 |
| Community and Social Services, Seniors Advocate | Cam Jackson | Room 117 NW<br>Legislative Building<br>Queen's Park, Toronto<br>Ontario, M7A-1A8 |
| Energy | Leo Jordan | Room 101 NW<br>Legislative Building<br>Queen's Park, Toronto<br>Ontario, M7A-1A8 |
| Housing, Culture and Communications, Disabled Advocate | Margaret Marland | Room 159<br>Legislative Building<br>Queen's Park, Toronto<br>Ontario, M7A-1A8 |
| Natural Resources, Mines | Allan McLean | Room 122 NW<br>Legislative Building<br>Queen's Park, Toronto<br>Ontario, M7A-1A8 |
| Municipal Affairs | Bill Murdoch | Room 165<br>Legislative Building<br>Queen's Park, Toronto<br>Ontario, M7A-1A8 |

| Portfolios | Name | Address |
|---|---|---|
| Solicitor General, Anti-Drug Strategy, Corrections | Bob Runciman | Room 104 NW, Legislative Building, Queen's Park, Toronto, Ontario, M7A-1A8 |
| Management Board, Greater Toronto Area | Chris Stockwell | Room 103 NW, Legislative Building, Queen's Park, Toronto, Ontario, M7A-1A8 |
| Consumer and Commercial Relations, Financial Institutions | David Tilson | Room 118 NW, Legislative Building, Queen's Park, Toronto, Ontario, M7A-1A8 |
| Transportation, Government Services | David Turnbull | Room 119 NW, Legislative Building, Queen's Park, Toronto, Ontario, M7A-1A8 |
| Agriculture, Francophone Affairs | Noble Villeneuve | Room 156, Legislative Building, Queen's Park, Toronto, Ontario, M7A-1A8 |
| Health | Jim Wilson | Room 123 NW, Legislative Building, Queen's Park, Toronto, Ontario, M7A-1A8 |
| Labour, Women's Issues | Elizabeth Witmer | Room 105 NW, Legislative Building, Queen's Park, Toronto, Ontario, M7A-1A8 |

 NOTES